"Angie's Miniature Challenges"
Magazine Projects

Part 1: 2000-2001

Dedication.

To the South Devon Dollshouse Club who first asked me to teach and to Marian Fancey who first challenged me to write articles. Thanks for the 'push'. XXXs

Publishing Data

First published 2014 Sliding Scale Books (SSPB02)

Plaza De Andalucia 1, Campofrio, 21668, Huelva, Spain.

(c) Copyright Angie Scarr 2000-2014
Text and step-by-step photography Angie Scarr 2000-2014
Additional photography Frank Fisher
Design by Frank Fisher and Angie Scarr

Sliding Scale SSPB02

All rights reserved
The right of Angie Scarr to be identified as the Author of this work has been asserted in accordance with the Copyright Designs and Patents Act 1988, sections 77 & 78.

No part of this publication may be reproduced, stored in a retrieval system or transmitted in any form or by any means without the prior permission of the publisher and author or her agents

The publishers and author can accept no legal responsibility for any consequences from the application of information instructions or advice given in this publication, or for errors, omissions or changes in formulae of mentioned materials.

Contents

Foreword, Introduction — 5
Foreword by Birdy Heywood and Introduction by Angie Scarr.

Wild Boar Head — 8
Capturing The Wild Boar.

Live Lobsters — 11
A Lobster Netted.

Pheasants — 14
A Brace Of Pheasants.

Pineapples — 17
Pineapples 3 Ways.

Squid — 20
Here's That Sick Squid You Asked For.

Eggs — 22
A Box Of Eggs.

Baked Potatoes — 25
One Potato, Two Potato, Three Potato.

Artichokes — 28
Or strange practices with kitchen utensils.

Tapas — 31
Viva España!

Alexandra Palace Fair — 35
Live At Ally Pally.

Sandwich — 38
Have We All Gone Mad!?

Red Cabbage — 41
I may have been leading her astray!

Sweets — 44
The Sweetest Things.

Tongue 47
Here's a killer only for the really very patient!

Peppers And Pizza 50
Where there's a will there's a way.

Tomatoes 53
Rather like seaside rock.

Moulded Fish 56
Sardines in crates quick sharp.

Strawberries 59
... or Jordgubbe.

Acknowledgements 62
And links to magazines

Index 63

"Angie's Miniature Challenges" Magazine Projects 2000-2005

Foreword by Birdy Heywood.

My first encounter with Angie Scarr was way back in the nineties at a craft show in London. At that time I was creating and selling little bears created from Polymer Clay. During a dinner break I wandered around the show and came across a stall surrounded by people. I eased my way to the front to see what they were all so interested in.

Boy was I impressed with what I saw as I had never experienced anything quite like it! There sat a woman surrounded by the most intricate examples of miniature food I had ever seen. Angie was demonstrating how to create slices of fish out of Polymer Clay. She explained each step to her on-lookers and I saw magic created before my very eyes as she reduced the cane, then sliced it into pieces. Absolute perfection! She told me that she had begun creating in 1991 and began teaching in 1995. I followed her progress and we met again in 1998 as tutors at a polymer clay event. By then she had produced a few videos on her techniques. She began writing a book in 1999 [Making Miniature Food ...] which I still have and have shared with others during workshops because I enjoyed the look of surprise on their faces when they delved inside and the comments like "What you mean to say that isn't real?"

Angie's instructions are so simple to follow in her books. Each stage has been expertly photographed and explained. A must have for miniaturists! A book written by The goddess of Miniature food. That is how high I rate her skills!

Angie is a true pioneer and one of the first people to lay the foundations for miniature artists who discovered polymer clay at a later date. Not only is she an expert demonstrator and designer but also a lovely personality who puts those at ease and willing to give it a go, people who have never even heard of polymer clay before.

www.birdyheywood.com
www.facebook.com/birdy.heywood

Introduction by Angie Scarr.

It seems strange looking back on 14 or 15 years of miniature project articles that when I first started writing them I had to use inverted commas round the words "Internet" and "surfing" and "capturing video" because when I started, the internet was something entirely new and I had had one of the few miniatures websites for a couple of years only by virtue of my husband Frank the "computer Geek" being so much of an aficionado at the time. Now I leave the strange way of explaining how I got hold of the pictures and information for my first few challenges as a testament to how quickly times have changed.

In producing this series of old articles as an ebook I am aware of the fact that many of the older miniaturists still may not have access to e-readers but they did have access to the original articles almost all of which are from editions now sold out. So I'm presenting these ideas to a whole new generation of miniaturists. When they were first published, most of the ideas were entirely or partly new. Now the techniques form part of how miniatures in polymer clay are done. Some have even been superseded by new methods either invented as improvements to my original ideas, or by other miniaturists.

One or two ideas were not my own, specifically the sweeties and the Jelly project. I had seen these done before I did them and unfortunately cannot credit because I'm not sure where I saw them. But my first kick-start in the very early 1990s was from seeing a lemon cane produced by an American artist I believe, I thought I knew how that was done so I went home and got out my polymer clay and had a go. I made a mistake in the technique and that led to me being able to re-enclose and peel the oranges I made. (I couldn't have done this using the original technique). This was a new idea at the time and I tried caning and re-enclosing all sorts of things. And making leaves with veins for cabbages and cauliflowers etc.

My Mum's friends asked me to show them how it was done and so the teaching started. When I sent my first three videos to Marian Fancey (owner and editor of Dolls House and Miniature scene at the time) she asked me if I would write a series of articles for them as their usual contributor on Polymer clay, Sue Heaser, was a little busy with her books. I told Marion that I was also writing a book but that as long as I could keep copyright, in case I wanted to include any of the ideas in the book, I would be very happy to write for them. I loved Marian's idea that the series should be of challenges sent in by the public, as I can never resist a challenge!

The larger part of this collection is of those challenges but I've also included articles originally published in other miniatures magazines and have mentioned the magazine in every case and issue number where I've been able to work that out. This collection has been partially revised and updated while leaving the 'essence' of the originals. As such, not every project gives the step-by-step instructions. In some cases a note about the way I now do things has been added, where it makes a significant improvement on the results. Many however are just a taste of the methods which are explored more thoroughly in my books. Where there is an important link to the books or to YouTube videos I have added these links to the text.

I hope you enjoy this look back at past challenges. I'm looking forward to writing more books in this format and to being able to present translations into other languages in the near future.

Please feel free to contact me with any comments or requests for information via my webform or on facebook

www.angiescarr.co.uk
facebook.com/angiescarr.miniatures
www.youtube.com/user/angiescarr

Best wishes, Angie.

"Angie's Miniature Challenges"
Magazine Projects

Part 1: 2000-2001

Boar's Head

Originally published in DHMS Magazine Issue 70 April 2000

Capturing The Wild Boar

This was set for me by Carol Barrass from Hull. Carol says she's having difficulty finding a really good boars head for a Tudor house. Carol receives the boars head pictured here as a gift from myself and DHMS. Thanks Carol for a really interesting challenge.

My first instinct, or rather that of my computer 'geek' husband Frank, was to look on the internet. By the way any of you who feel I'm being rather insulting to my husband should understand that 'geek' is a term of respect to the real computer expert. So we 'surfed' all over the web. We found some pretty gruesome hunting pictures. Some of which appeared to have tusks...I just became more confused. What is the difference between a pig, a boar and a hog anyway? Who would eat these and when. And particularly, what would boar's head be served on? A wooden trencher perhaps, maybe pewter?

Then we noticed a medieval banquet was being served on the Christmas 'Time Team' programme. Sure enough they were serving boar's head. We videoed the episode and I tried hard to study the picture carefully but of course pausing video never quite works. Once again the 'geek' proved his worth. He has access to a program called video capture which turns ordinary video film into a series of digital stills. So last weekend we sallied off to our computer club and literally captured ourselves a boar!

I was surprised to see that the boar's head was served on a wicker basket, but I couldn't see any tusks! It was however decorated simply with herbs which I recognised as a wreath of bayleaves and rosemary in the ears and behind the head. I decided I needed more information.

I asked Aileen of Merry Gourmet Miniatures who is fascinating to talk to and something of a fount of knowledge when it comes to the history of food. This is what she told me. Pigs and hogs were domesticated animals and would be likely to be kept and eaten by peasants but not served as a whole head on a platter.

The wild boar was a trophy from hunting which was prohibited to the peasants and gruesome punishments could befall the poacher. Therefore boar's head was only served in the highest class households and for special occasions only. It was a popular celebratory centrepiece dish for many centuries from early mediaeval through Elizabethan times, perhaps beyond. The methods of serving would be different in the different periods according to Aileen. During mediaeval times the dish would be more highly decorated using gilding apparently they even prepared foods to look as if they were something else perhaps minced meat would be rolled into balls, to look like a gilded apple. Their banqueting could be very ornate. I finally decided on a simple version like the Time Team one, since Aileen assures me that actually the Tudor serving would be the simpler. The serving dish was still threatening to be a problem for me. Aileen also answered this for me. Again, since it was a dish for the rich I could chose between gold silver, pewter etc. and could, if I wished, ignore the humbler...but more difficult wicker and the wooden trencher for which I just don't have the necessary woodworking skills.

I did both. A wicker basket with all the herbs and ...

Here's a simple version for you to try.

Step 1

Firstly you need 3cm cone shape of cream coloured polymer clay and two small triangles for the ears. Cut off the end and form a snout shape. Nip in and flatten the forehead & top of the snout. Give it a little edge by tweaking the end.

Step 2

Mark a line down the centre of the snout and add the nostrils. Also mark the eyes simply just to give you an idea where to put the ears. add the ears in a curve from just behind the eyes.

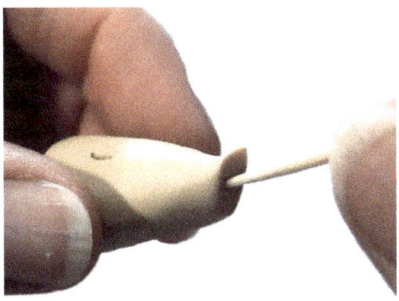

Step 3

Cut the mouth from just behind the snout about 1cm long. Deepen the eye sockets around the eyes but make sure they have a closed appearance unless you're feeling particularly macabre! Wild

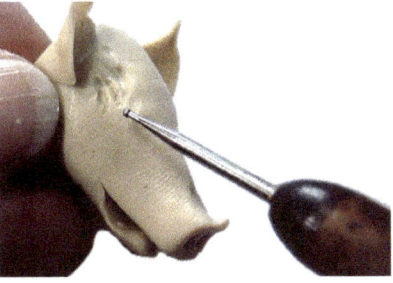

boars do have a sort of ridge where the tusk lines up with the upper jaw. I left these out for simplicity but for extra realism you could add a little extra clay here

gently smooth the clay around it to build the edges up slightly. Finally cut the mouth from just behind the snout back by about a centimetre. Put an apple (pale green) or onion shape (translucent & very pale green mix) into the mouth and finally two tiny cones of pale cream upwards from each side of the mouth for the tusks.

Push some 'mix quick' or translucent clay firmly onto your oval dish. *[These days I use Liquid Fimo to attach items to plates etc.]* Gently press the boar head onto this base.

Step 4

To form the leaves you can use leaf green or a sandwich of leaf green and a lighter green mix. Cut out tiny leaf shapes as illustrated opposite.

Step 5

Pinch together into pairs and form a line down the centre of each with a cocktail stick or dental tool.

Step 6

Roll some darker green into very fine stems and attach a few leaves. Make two or three of these and pre cook them. (This is so they will stand up behind the head.)

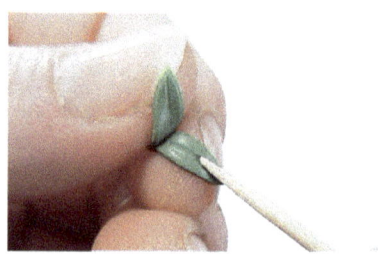

Step 7

Add more leaves around the edge of the platter. Try to make sure some of your leaves overlap the edge of the dish. After you have oven set the boar's head you can add the cooked highly glazed look with

Humbrol Clear Colour. *[Humbrol Clear Colour may not be available now, so just use ochre and brown colour pastels or powder and varnish]*

Step 8

If you have very nimble fingers you can make the little flower buds for the bay leaves but this isn't strictly necessary as they only flower in the winter season. In the spring there would be new lighter green growths but that's really going too far. So it's the sort of thing I'd do!

Are you 'boared' yet?

Originally published in DHMS Magazine Issue 71 May 2000

Live Lobsters

A Lobster Netted

Anyone who knows me well knows how I hate Lobsters! No, I'm sure they're lovely little critters and highly edible but they're murder to make.

So here's a really difficult challenge set for me by Lesley Symonds of Braunton

Miniaturists Club, who once waited two years for one of my cooked lobsters. Lesley, for incredible patience Here are a pair of uncooked lobsters. And to make sure they don't get away a pot to keep them in!

Well, do you know the difference between a blue lobster and an uncooked lobster? Someone told me uncooked lobsters were blue so I went web surfing again to 'net' me a lobster. Of course I put in the keywords lobster +blue. Sure enough there were pages and pages about blue lobsters. They turned out to be a species of freshwater lobster, related but not the same as our traditional pink when cooked variety. Then I found a fascinating (yawn) webcam page of live lobsters. For anyone who doesn't understand the internet that's a sort of live 'paint drying' experience. It wasn't exactly informative. I could see that they were greyish but that was about all.

Would you believe it was channel 4 who provided me yet again with the answer. Straight after Time Team, which had previously yielded the elusive boar's head, came the quirky Hugh Fearnley-Wittingstall and his Return to River Cottage. Hugh went lobster fishing and took away a generously sized uncooked lobster. after wisely binding his claws with rubber bands. Again I got a couple of good still shots from a video capture. Ahh how I love technology.

I shall miss HFW more for the recent series than for his placenta pate programme from the TV dinners series which incidentally featured an acquaintance of mine. Yes, a strange and unnerving programme. Proving that I have even stranger friends than miniaturists! I had thought of doing the whole scene with Hugh and his salty old seadog friend examining the catch. But I couldn't work out how to make a HFW doll look any different from Johnathan Creek!

I went back to the internet to find out the history of lobster consumption and to check that lobsters would be at home in any doll's house. I got back as far as Anglo Saxon times. I guess that means that a lobster could turn up in any dollshouse kitchen.

As far as I could find out lobster pot designs vary but the one that Hugh used was fairly much a traditional British design which has changed little in centuries. It also seems that we're taking very small lobsters from the water these days. (No surprise there then.) There's a 1934 painting by Fred Elwell called The Fish Stall which is held by the Bury Art Gallery. It depicts a stallholder offering lobsters at least twice the size of those I'm used to seeing. That's my excuse for the size of my lobsters and I'm sticking to it. Although I used very complex caning to produce the dappled carapace on my 'challenge' lobster, here's an easier version for you to try. Please forgive my painting, paint really isn't my medium.

I also have a video of this on my YouTube channel, and a mould to make it easier. Go to my website angiescarr.co.uk for links to both

Step 1

Start with two very thin rolls of cream coloured polymer clay for the feelers. I used a mix of champagne and white Fimo. And I added a little Mix Quick for flexibility. Curl over the ends and pre cook these with two tiny eye stalks. Make

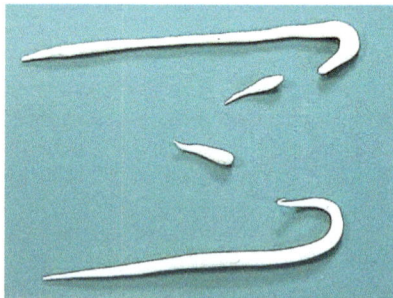

these as a long but very tiny teardrop shape. Bake these first, they will be pushed into the body when they have been hardened.

Step 2

You then need a large teardrop shape for the body and two slightly smaller for the claws. You'll also need four very thin leg pieces.

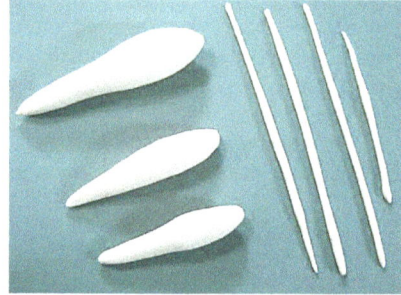

Step 3

Make the head end pointed and flatten the tail. Make markings as in the photographs. Try to do this confidently, as attempting to be over precise usually means making a hash of it! I used a ball ended tool available at sugarcraft shops.

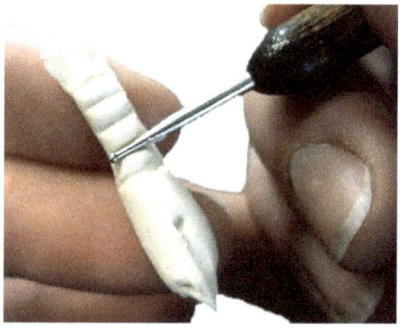

Step 4

Press the end of the claw section to flatten it and press the sugarcraft tool into it to mark where the claw hinges.

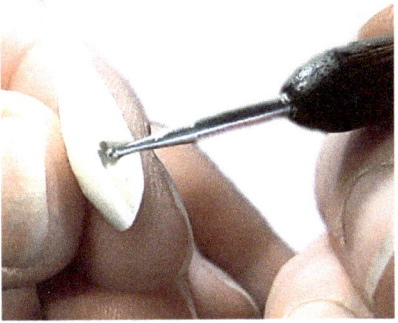

Step 5

Press the tool firmly through the material to separate the claw and mark the serrations.

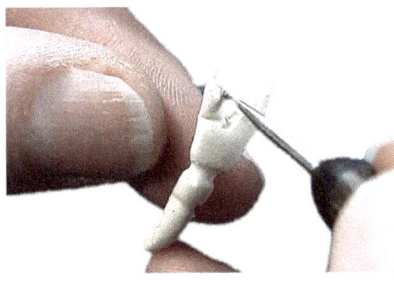

Step 6

Assemble the parts as shown, uncurled. Add the feelers and eyes and curl the legs under and slightly forward. Then tuck the tail up under the body (or you could leave it uncurled) and oven set the lobster.

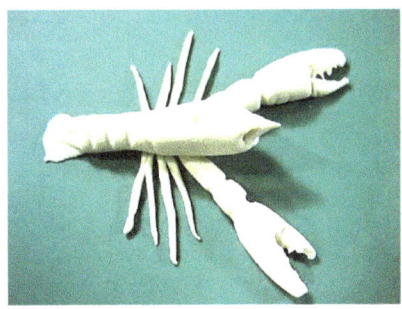

Step 7

Paint using a stippling action. Brown paint on the sides first and finally use a little black lightly stippled onto the back. Put a little black on the tips of the eye stalks and the feelers. I recommend using only a very light coating of varnish to make it look damp but not over shiny.

The netting is between £1-2 a metre at fabric shops and you only need a very little, wetted and scrunched for this display.

Just a few tiny shells complete the scene.

Pheasants

Originally published in DHMS Magazine Issue 72 June 2000

A Brace Of Pheasants

Thank you all for your interesting challenges, the first of which I'll cover next month. Meanwhile, I've lost count of the times I've been asked for furry and feathered items. This is a real challenge for me

to create the look of something so natural with what is essentially a 'plastic'. These are for Alison Taylor of Oxford. A special pleasure for me because Alison is in fact my cousin and a very creative lady herself.

I decided to do these for the real experts but I hope they will inspire those of you who are just getting into polymer clay. This challenge just shows how complex caning can become. 'Caning' is the building up of colours into strips which can be lengthened later. It's rather like a seaside rock maker builds the tiny letters into his rock by making them short and fat first and then lengthens them cutting the resultant canes into both large and small sticks of rock.

For those who are new to caning there are some reasonably simple caning projects in the Projects magazine article (1998 v2) that covers weddings.

Or you can find an oranges project on my website angiescarr.co.uk and there are also links there to YouTube videos of various items.

Step 1

Incidentally when you have made a cane you can keep it almost indefinitely, The eye cane from the male pheasant shown here is well over a year old. It's one of those projects I started but never finished....as you do. You don't even need to keep it in an airtight container. I use video boxes which are an ideal way to store parts for later assembly. sometimes you have to warm and squeeze an old cane a little to resurrect it, but the most important thing is to try to keep them out of strong sunlight and fluctuating temperatures.

If you don't want to do all the caning

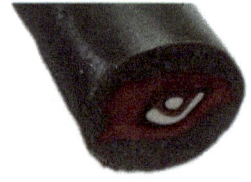

you can just get the basic colours right and chop them finely, shape the pheasants body and use a dental tool or toothpick to scratch in the texture.

Step 2

Usually I advise people to buy the real object wherever possible but most of my challenges are fairly rare items and pheasants are no exception.

So, this seems like a good opportunity to introduce you to my Bible.
'The Book of Ingredients'
ISBN-13: 978-0718130435.
I really think the publishers should be paying me royalties I recommend it so highly! It's a photographic record of many of the raw materials we use in cooking. Including sections on fish, meats fruit and vegetables, poultry and game. The photographs are either full size or to a stated scale. I used the photographs of pheasants to investigate the colours, shapes and sizes of both the male and female pheasant.

Step 3

I also bought some pheasant feathers at Focus which no longer exists, but try other hobby shops. This allowed me to

look really closely at the patterns in each feather. I found out there were about four main types of patterns with slight variations. Here I show you how I copied just one complicated feather pattern.

Funnily enough although most people think of the female pheasant as the plainer the feathers are in fact equally complex and beautiful.

Step 4

Build up the complex canes by cutting the original cylinders into tessellating fish scale shapes

Step 5

and when you have several styles of feather they can be added together to make a large complicated cane

Step 6

you use slices of the result to wrap around the body.

Step 7

My advice is to make the heads first onto a long 'stalk' of neck and oven set them first. This is for the male pheasant.

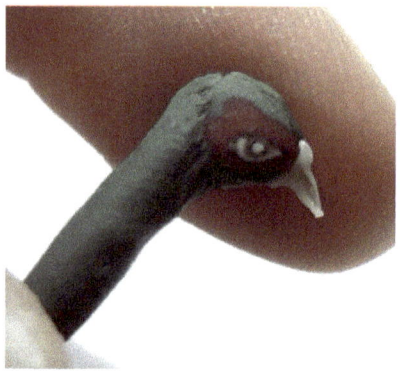

Step 8

At the same time you need to make some skinny legs and tail feathers.

Next build a smallish body shape with mix quick or a soft polymer clay, and do the same with the legs.

Step 9

Wrap your thin slices around the body and the leg sections and attach the legs to the body. You can then add extra 'feathers' to build up a wing if you wish. I cheat and just indent it slightly.

Step 10

Finally I ruin all my hard work by texturing it a little with a dental tool! Yes this is an absolutely crazy way to do it ... But that's me! This picture is of the female feather cane, you do want a brace, right?

There is another way to make feathers from polymer clay involving scratching clay off a block but you wouldn't want to hear about that would you? Keep those challenges coming.

Pineapples

Originally published in DHMS Magazine Issue 73 July 2000

Pineapples 3 Ways

I have had several requests for pineapples, Obviously a source of much frustration to many of you. Julia Smart says:- "The best I could do looked like a hand grenade!"

And Margaret Cassidy asks me for "one that I could cut open, one that looks really juicy and good enough to eat." Margaret and Julia I'm happy to oblige.

Looking for the history of this beautiful and delicious fruit I thought I'd ask the man most obviously in the know. But this time according to the Internet there were some missing web pages. Although the headers were tantalisingly there, hinting at a history as a favourite of the nobility, the man from DelMonte he said no! I did find from a different Internet page that King Charles had his portrait painted receiving a pineapple (symbolic of royal privilege) as a gift. So, my search wasn't entirely fruitless. (groan)

According to my favourite food historian (Aileen Tucker of course) the first pineapple to be raised successfully in Britain (and possibly the same one) was presented to King Charles in 1720. The gardener responsible had, apparently, used a 'hot pit' a process of producing heat by fermenting bark chippings. It may be that the gardener responsible had as many attempts and failures as I had producing the twelfth scale version.

Although available to the big houses in late Victorian times after the advent of refrigerated ships, pineapples continued to be a fairly exotic fruit realistically until around the 1960s. I certainly don't remember seeing them in my local village shops as a child, and I was born in '57. Of course tinned pineapple rings will have been available for some time by the turn of the (last) century, due to canning.

Step 1

All the leaves are made by the same method as in issue 71 with the boars head article. In case you missed it that is by cutting out a circle of green and then using the same circle cutter to cut a leaf shape

nal lines, i.e. top right to bottom left all the way round. Then top left to bottom right. This gives a sort of art nouveau carved pineapple effect after the paint has been added. *[See also the new method introduced in the artichokes challenge later]*

Step 3

Or you could make a mould as I have here. I truly wish I could find out the name of the little tree took the 'pattern' from. I don't even know if it was a flower or a fruit. It just looks like a tiny green pine cone

from the edge. Use florists wire with a blob of mix quick as a sticky base to attach the leaves to. Before you oven set them, dust the back of the leaves with talcum powder or chalk powder to give the lightened look that is on real pineapples. Cook these in advance and then cut the wire short and poke it into the top of your chosen type of pineapple.

Here are three pineapple methods for you to try according to your abilities, or as Mr Geek (my husband) puts it your 'mad miniaturist' quotient.

Step 2

The 'hand grenade' method. probably the one Julia came unstuck with. You need a small piece of orange polymer clay. With a cocktail stick, dental tool or I used a scalpel (Careful!) indent two sets of parallel diago-

or, as I thought, a twelfth scale pineapple. If anyone knows, please put us out of our misery! When you find one, as I'm sure you all will, make your mould it the same day as they dry out very quickly.

I've used Milliput to make the mould, and a thin layer of Humbrol Maskol to cover the pattern and between the two halves of the mould. You mix enough Milliput to sink one side of the 'pattern' into. When it has hardened paint on a layer of Maskol and add the second side. When the Milliput has hardened prise the two sides apart and take out the pattern. I have plans to use and show this method of mould making fully in a future challenge. I now use Minitmold, available from my website, for most of my moulding, as it sets very quickly.

With both these methods you'll need to use green paint to separate the diamond shapes. to do this paint some acrylic paint between the sections and quickly use a soft cloth to rub it off again. This should leave

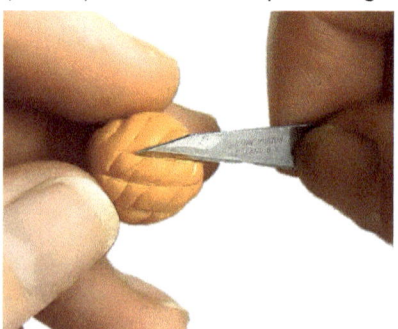

just enough paint as a green 'lowlight.' You could use a miniature drill buffer to help polish the paint off the surface.

Step 4

The third method is of course the really crazy caning method.

Step 5

If you are an old hand at caning you should get the idea from the pictures.

Step 6

The centre of the pineapple is actually fairly simple. I used some original yellow translucent Fimo (unfortunately only available now in Fimo soft) and porcelain Doll Fimo to make the stripes. Or you could use a translucent/white mix. If you can't get hold of yellow translucent Fimo you can simply add a tiny bit of golden yellow to plain translucent. I stacked the colours up (see the onions project in my book Making Miniature Food or go to my website for the YouTube link). Add a little Fimo glaze to make it look really juicy.

YouTube!

On my website angiescarr.co.uk there is a link to my YouTube videos on how to make pineapples.
www.youtube.com/user/angiescarr

Squid

Originally published in DHMS Magazine Issue 74 August 2000

Here's that sick squid you asked for Margaret!

How could I resist taking up Miss Margaret's challenge when we met at the Pudsey fair in April? Margaret asked for another of our fishy friends the Squid.

Margaret offered to do one of her wonderfully embroidered logos for me. So Margaret I think that's worth sick squid! (pun intended).

Thank you also to my local fishmonger on Hessle road, which is historically the centre of the fishing community in Hull. Mr Simpson told me that Squid are very common around the shores of Britain and could be found on any table in almost any period of history. This was news to me as I'd always thought of it as rather an exotic dish.

The main problem I had when making Squid was getting the translucency right and the colour on the skin thin enough. Again, like Lobsters you could just lightly paint the whole thing but for a really good finish you can't beat making it all with Polymer clay.

Step 1

Here I've used porcelain Doll Fimo for the main body colour, it has just the right qualities, however you can mix a 75% to 25% Translucent / White mix which should do just as well since the Doll Fimo is rather difficult to find and comes in very large and

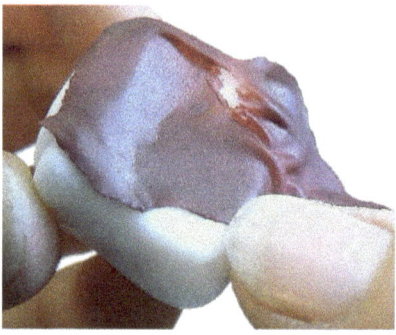

expensive packs. Other makes of polymer clay have varying translucencies, but generally the mix will be somewhat similar.

The skin is created by making the very thinnest sheet you possibly can of a burgundy colour. Place a really small piece over a cube of conditioned (hand softened) clay

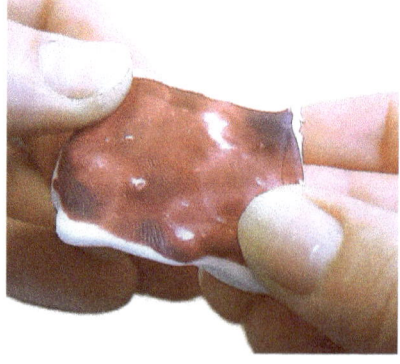

Step 2

Press together until the material really stretches to its limit and the white starts to show through where it begins to crack. Roll this sheet into a 'log' (cane) and lengthen it until it is only about one half centimetre wide.

Step 3

Repeat the whole process using a darker purply black. Cut the first cane and pinch the colour over one end. Cut off this cone shape. Using a ball ended tool or a sanded off cocktail stick make a hollow in the bottom of the cone. Push a similar or slightly smaller cone into this hollow.

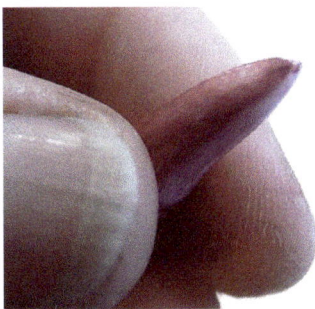

Step 4

Using a ball ended tool hollow the body where the legs will go.

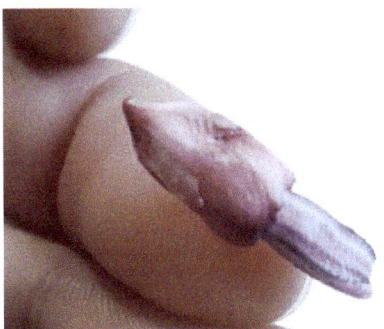

Step 5

Using a dental tool or a fairly blunt blade form the legs rolling one into a longer strip.

Step 6

Pinch the two 'wing' areas and subtly mark in a central line Add two tiny eyes with the darker colour. Oven set on a plate or ceramic tile or on its final display.

Step 7

For instance you could make your own marble slab out of Fimo by mixing a little grey and black roughly into white by chopping them together. Then roll and chop the material a couple of times until it resembles marble. Roll this mix into a fairly thin sheet on a ceramic tile. Then cut into rectangles using a ruler or set square but do not try to remove from your tile. After setting the material you can then remove it from the tile and finish by sanding the edges to soften them. You will find glazing with Fimo varnish will give the squid its wet and slimy look but be careful not to overdo this. You could try mixing matt and gloss varnishes for just the right look.

Eggs

Originally published in DHMS Magazine Issue 75 September 2000

A Box Of Eggs

Thanks to Margaret Bird who I met at Hove for asking me for egg trays, and to Mike Bennett who requested eggs among an arm's length list. (Ooh Mike, that's cheating!)

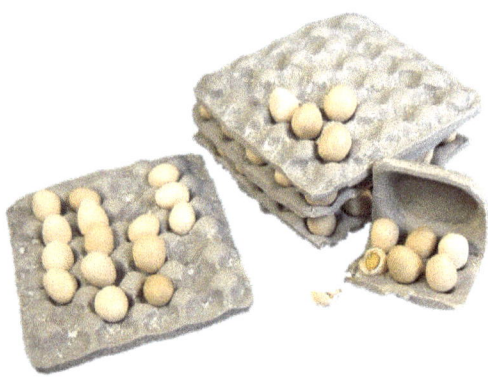

I also have to thank the lovely lady I met on the bus who admits she'll be 80 next birthday. Isn't it strange how we start to admit our age again after three score and ten. She (Ethel?) had worked in a grocery and filled me in on how the farmers used to bring baskets of eggs to sell in Hull from south of the river (Humber) as well as all over East Yorkshire, since there was a paddle steamer crossing in those days. I asked her when she first remembered papier mache egg trays and boxes. She said not until after the war. She tried to explain the earlier wooden boxes with card sectional inserts unfortunately I only half understood. If anyone has details of these early egg boxes perhaps you would write in to the magazine and let us know.

This was a fairly difficult challenge for me as I'm a bit of a novice at mould making and I'm sure that I break all the rules. In this project I used Milliput to make any moulds I needed, it is available at most good model shops and comes in several colours. The cheapest and I think the best for moulds is the standard grey although I've used white here as that is what I have available at home. Milliput is a two part epoxy type material and you should use thin gloves when working it. You will find that it sticks a little as you are mixing it but you can wash your hands with the gloves on as when it's fresh it is soluble in water. Mix only the very small amounts you require as it hardens spontaneously some time after mixing.

To make moulds by this method you will have to have great patience or only fifteen minutes a day to spare, as each part of the process is short but takes a day to harden. *[I now use Minitmold, available from my website angiescarr.co.uk, for most of my moulding, as it sets in about 10 minutes and doesn't need a release agent, other than a little talcum powder to make the second part of a mould.]*

Step 1

Firstly you need to form a shallow rectangle of Milliput and with a highlighter pen press gently twice side by side to form two indentations. One will form the lid and one the base of the egg box. You can smooth these and tidy them up with a modelling tool and a little water. I use a washing up sponge in a mug about a third full of water. I constantly damp my modelling tools. The effect is smoother and therefore forms a better mould. Leave this part to set overnight.

Step 2
Next day add a little more Milliput to half of the box shape.

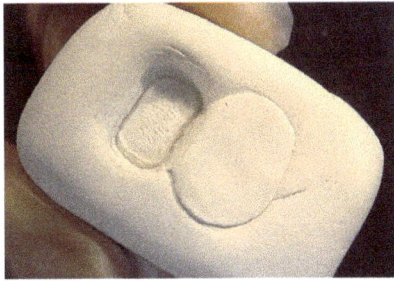

Step 3
Now you indent this with a 'posidriv' type screwdriver (I use just the attachment). You must take care that the cross head runs parallel to the box sides. That is to say that it forms a + and not an X.

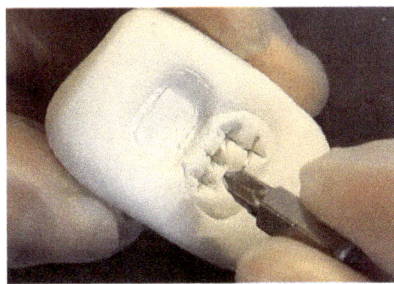

Step 4
With a narrow flat ended modelling tool press back each of the 'envelope' sections of the + to form the egg holders. Then put an edge around the mould to give you an idea of the cutting edge. Harden this section.

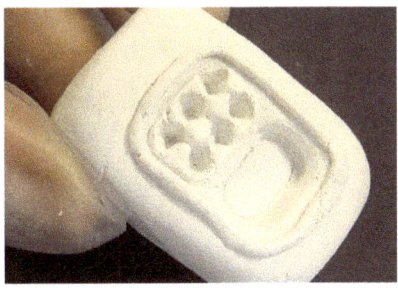

Step 5
Incidentally you can make your egg trays by using a crosshead screwdriver in the same way. This one was made using Fimo.

Step 6
Next day paint the whole thing with a thick coat of Maskol.

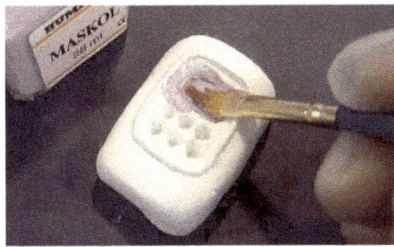

Step 7

and when this has dried push some more Milliput into the mould to form the top section. It is advisable to give this a finger grip to help you pull the finished mould apart. A day later, when this has hardened, draw some locating arrows on each half of the mould, pull apart and remove the Maskol.

Step 8

Mix a pale grey polymer clay and roll out fairly thin sheets. Press them slightly into the mould and finish off by pushing the two halves gently but firmly together. I use talc as a freeing agent.

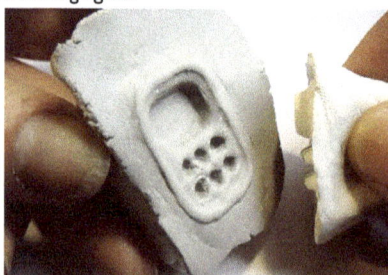

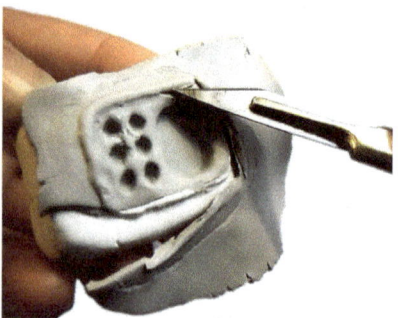

Step 9

If you were making trays you could take the whole thing out of the mould at this stage and place on a plate or ceramic tile. When you make egg boxes you need to trim them and oven set them still inside the mould.

Step 10

Take them out carefully while they are still hot and gently fold together inside a tea towel or cloth. As they cool they retain a half closed shape. Eggs are a little obvious but to add some humour you could make a tiny broken egg as I have here.

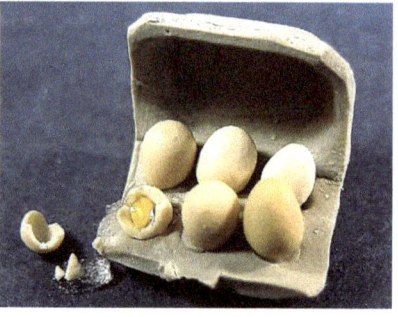

Step 11

With a ball ended tool press into a tiny ball of clay to form an open egg shape. Set this, then, using nail scissors cut little bits out to simulate the broken edge. You need to put a tiny bit of yellow Fimo to look like the yolk and cook it again. finally when you are making your display add some 'Scenic Water' I bought mine at a miniatures fair *[or now I use Liquid Fimo]*. With eggtrays, don't forget to stack up several layers. Of course you don't have to have eggs all the way through so you can make the edge ones and stick the whole tray on top of another using Mix Quick, or leftover Fimo as long as its fresh.

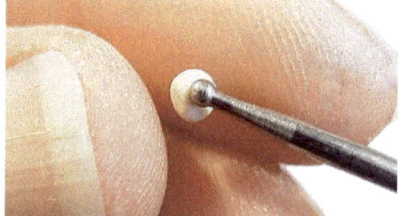

Baked Potatoes

Originally published in DHMS Magazine Issue 77 November 2000

One Potato, Two Potato, Three Potato

Many thanks, as always to the reader who challenged me to baked potatoes. Nikki Belgrove came up with this nice simple idea which I haven't made before. This gave me the opportunity to introduce a few more potato ideas as well. Nikki's sister Sarah asked me if I could make paella. Mmm Sarah. I think I'll just go and do a little

research on location!

The basic potato mix is (approximately) 50% translucent. 25% white and 25% cream coloured Fimo with just a tiny scrap of ochre.

Step 1
One Potato....

Firstly you need to roll a tiny oval shape approximately 1cm long for a large-ish baked potato. Roll this potato before hardening on a piece of sponge dipped in brown acrylic paint. I've used Humbrol's 'matt dark earth'.

Step 2

Before you cook the potato you need to cut it in a cross shape and gently open it out with your blade. I then pre-cooked it so I could make the butter look melted on it without squashing the potato. For the butter I've used a mix of yellow, cream and translucent Fimo. The coleslaw is just grated Fimo consisting largely of a translucent/white mix with just a little scraping of pale orange and pale green mixes.

Step 3

You'll need the grater with the smallest holes that you can find. Mine came from Ikea and of course I keep it only for modelling and not for the kitchen. Next month I'll show you an even more unusual use for common kitchen tools!

By the way the methods for making the eggs and cucumbers and also the beef pictured with the mashed potato have appeared in Projects magazine (the Wedding issue).

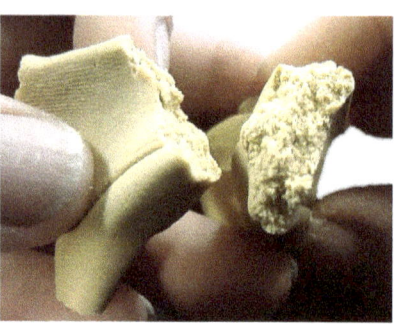

Step 4

Two potato....

Chips. Easy peasy! Just use the same potato mix, cut tiny chip shapes and stack together. Avoid squashing the nice sharp edges and don't paint the glaze on until after you have set the clay.

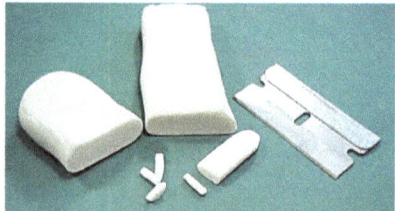

Step 5

The battered fish uses the same method of texturing the clay as I employ for 'mash'. I simply pull the material apart fairly sharply and just touch up the texture with a dental tool. You could even use the same method for mushy peas!

Step 6

Then simply take a slice with the blade.

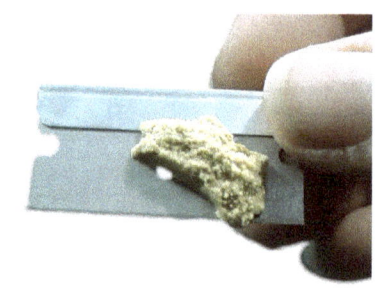

Step 7

Mr Geek (my affectionate name for my computer obsessed husband) made the newspaper, by using my digital camera for a photo of a real newspaper article. An improvement on my photocopy reduction process I think. *[Obviously if you have a scanner that is easier still]*

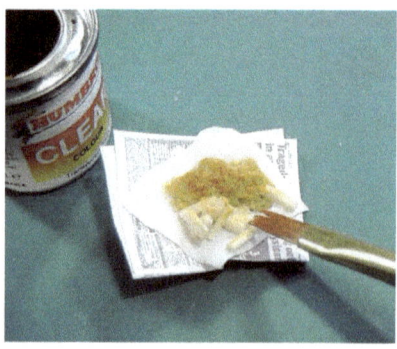

Step 8
Three potato...

Mash. Well at least you don't have to peel the potatoes. Of course you could ... just make the potato as you did for the baked, and rip the potato clay apart as you did to create the batter texture for the fish, and simply cut pieces off it.

Step 9
Four...?

They're not shown but don't forget to try making roast potatoes, just like the chips but cut little oval potatoes into quarters. You can use them to dress up your Christmas turkeys (see the Ally Pally challenge) or roast meat dishes.

Artichokes

Originally published in DHMS Magazine Issue 78 December 2000

Or strange practices with kitchen utensils

This must be how it feels when an athlete breaks his own 'record breaking' record. Oh how I hate to admit it but everything I've done in the past now looks so ridiculous and overcomplicated. While searching for a way to make artichokes

for Nikki Belgrove I've stumbled upon the only really sensible way to make pineapples. So, can I rewind and do that again please Marion?

I hit upon the idea of using a sieve as a texturing tool to produce the leaves on artichokes. The idea came to me, as these things usually do, in bed on a Sunday morning. That's the time my imagination is allowed to run wild. Of course that meant that Sunday afternoon was spent dragging Mr Geek around the supermarkets to find sieves with different sizes of mesh.

Here's an important little tip. The cheaper the item, the wider the mesh size! So my supermarket buys were all very well but rather too good quality. On Monday I was back out again trawling the sort of shops where if it isn't three for a pound they don't sell it, for the cheapest, but for me not the nastiest kitchen utensils available.

Step 1

The little basket (left) shows the products of three of my 'finds'.

Step 2

The largest mesh sieve produced the artichoke. Then of course I was hooked and decided to see what else I could produce using the rest of my finds. That's when I put my head in my hands and realised what a fool I'd been. The pineapples were incredibly simple by this method with a medium sized mesh. And with the

tiniest mesh, in this case a splatter guard I managed to produce passable pine cones.

Step 3

To produce the texture you need to press the polymer clay fairly firmly through the mesh, but only by a millimetre or so. Then you carefully peel it back out again. You may have to practise this a few times.

Step 4

Then you slice a thin slice from the surface. In the case of the artichoke the slice needs the top folding over and then the whole thing wrapping round a central stem cylinder so that the top is reasonably flat.

Step 5

I then hardened them and slightly carved where the head of the artichoke met the body. I used a piece of burgundy coloured clay rubbed over the surface of the top to colour it very subtly and then cooked it again. You can, of course dust it

with powder colours but I didn't have any of the correct colour at the time.

Step 6

Pineapples ... again

The Pineapple leaves were made by the same method, indeed at the same time as the ones in the pineapples challenge (DHMS 74)

Step 7

and again the skin was wrapped round a central core.

Incidentally, I've been asked many times since that article came out, how I produced the pineapple flesh. Quite simply I made a stack of translucent/yellow mix polymer clay and a translucent/white mix. (Stacking techniques are in my videos) I then wrapped the stripy 'stack' around a central core of very slightly more orangey mix. and formed a cane about a centimetre or so in diameter. The core was of course cut out again for the pineapple slices.

Step 8

The tiny pine cones were a really small thin slice from the surface of a textured piece of clay wrapped again round a very small cylinder piece.

Examples of other kitchen tools I've used for miniaturing include a pasta maker, a grater (last month's challenge), a food processor (for mixing large amounts of clay), serrated knives, cake decorating tools - the list goes on. In fact there's very little left in my kitchen. But that doesn't matter much as, since I moved house and have been building walls in between writing my book and rising to these challenges, I've only time for takeaways! Yes my polymer clay addiction is matched only by my chocoholism. Has anyone else noticed the fish scale texture in the bottom of a box of matchmakers? So don't blame me when your husband or wife finds the garlic press under your bed! (or is that just me?)

I've also got to find time this weekend to make complicated friendship beads for my local community fete. I've got to write 'Coltman Street Village 2000' in it, like a stick of seaside rock. Now that is a challenge. So ... where's my 'chipper'?

Tapas

Originally published in DHMS Magazine Issue 79 Jan 2001

Viva España!

This is the time of year when you're getting sick of Christmas from every shop window and every magazine and TV programme. So, if you're browsing your favourite miniatures magazine for ideas to trigger your creativity why not try recreating happy summer holidays to cheer away those midwinter blues.

I promised Sarah Belgrove that I would tackle paella when I had chance to do a little investigation. Actually, I already had plans for our first proper holiday in three years so any old excuse was enough.

I've been lucky enough to visit southern Spain three times, I'm now considering creating my own tapas bar and just sitting back and fantasising. For now here are my ideas for the two items which I have been challenged to make, and a few more ideas for authentic Spanish cuisine.

Paella is not the most common item on the restaurant menu in Andalucia, and my husband is vegetarian so we spent a lot of time trundling round trying to find a pizza restaurant, a bit of a waste of good culture sampling time in my opinion.

The southern Spanish are particularly carnivorous, especially enjoying all types of seafood, prawns, shellfish, squid and even octopus being commonly eaten. The other most common foods are somewhat greasy cheeses (no doubt suffering from the heat) and 'Jamon' a dry cured (uncooked) ham rather like Parma ham which is served freshly cut from the bone in every bar and restaurant and which to me is the taste of Andalucia.

For a really authentic tapas bar scene you shouldn't forget the olive stones and scrunched up tissues on the floor!

Step 1

An acceptable olive colour can be produced with a mix of leaf green and a little orange. Gradually add more orange to make at least two or preferably three variants of the basic colour. Mixing several

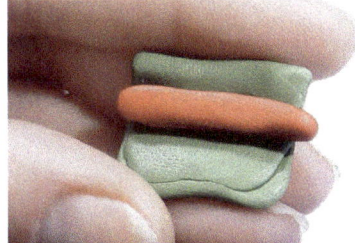

shades in this way produces a more realistic result than making them all the same shade. I made the olives 'stuffed' with red for pimentos as this was my challenge and also more colourful. In a Spanish bar however you are more likely to find plain olives perhaps even with their stalks still on, or olives drenched with olive oil crushed garlic and herbs. It is a little fiddly making the tiny little olives.

Step 2

Following my usual route I made a cane with red in the middle,

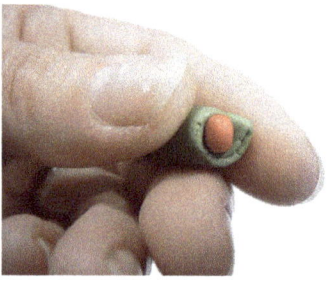

Step 3

then rounded off one end and cut these off 'tweaking' the other end to form the oval shape with the slightly indented end.

Of course you could just take the easy route and paint the red on, or just put a little dint in the visible end of half of them. Don't be fooled into thinking you should put a hole and a cross in the other end if you're doing the Spanish version, since you will almost never find stoned olives in a bar.

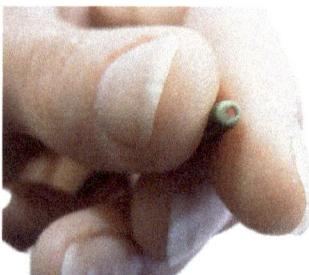

Step 4

The paella pan is much easier to make than you would think. Since it is black and the contents are brightly coloured you can get away with minor imperfections. I simply cut a circle with a sugarcraft cutter a little larger than a 10p piece but any size will do as long as you can find a coin to fit within it. Paella pans come in many sizes!

Step 5

I gently pressed the edges of the circles up the sides of the coin and placed this coin downwards on to a cooking surface.

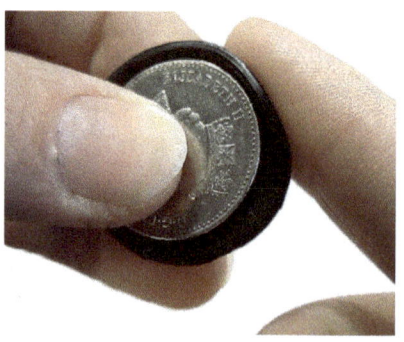

Step 6

Then I rolled two tiny cylinders for handles and pressed them up to the edge of the 'pan' with a modelling tool. This pan was first oven hardened and left to cool.

Step 7

The rice mix was a yellow white and translucent mix simply torn apart as I did with the potato and the fish batter in the baked potatoes challenge in issue 77

Step 8

I stuck the 'rice' to the previously cooked pan with a little Mix Quick.

Tiny green peas and little shreds of red for peppers brightened this base. Then I added the fishy bits.

Step 9

For the garnish, first I made the squid rings from doll white Fimo. (75% translucent 25% white would do) I cut the rings from this roll still on the needle.

The prawns were from my own stock *[on my Youtube channel there is a video on how to make prawns. Find the link on my website angiescarr.co.uk]*

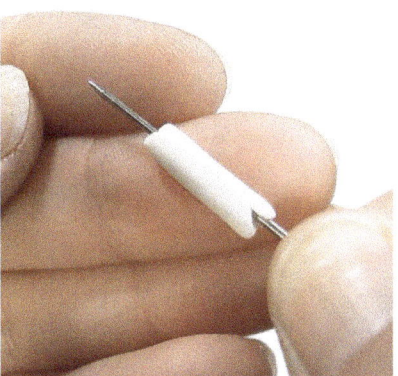

Step 10

I made the mussel shells from a thin slice each of black, and a grey made from black and the same translucent/white mix, or doll porcelain colour.

 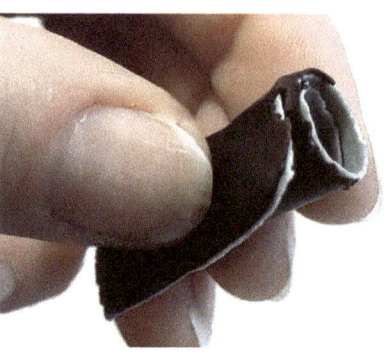

Step 11

rolled up into a teardrop shaped cane and sliced, with little mussels made from a mix of cream, orange and ochre.

Step 12

After cooking I added a little golden glaze round the edge to make it look cooked. The olives I varnished so they looked as if they were in oil and added some scenic scatter for herbs.

Just for the display I added a basket of bread and the little bread sticks served in every bar and restaurant in Spain. I must admit that on our holiday for the most part these baskets were returned entirely untouched by my family but they do look nice.

Alexandra Palace Fair

Originally published in DHMS Magazine Issue 80 Feb 2001

Live At Ally Pally

First of all a big thank you to everyone who visited my demonstration stand at the Alexandra Palace Fair and left so many in-

teresting challenges, some of which I'll get round to in the next few months. Also my apologies for my below par performance at the evening dinner where fatigue had left me rather 'musically challenged'. I think the matches holding up my eyelids must have slipped! Yup, the dog tired life of a full-time

miniaturist ... ahh aint that the blues.

I had asked for ideas for a 'live challenge' that I would attempt each day at 2pm as well as smaller requests and questions throughout the day. Some of the ideas were difficult to do without an on site oven to set the pieces between processes and some needed a little thinking about. However we all seemed to be feeling rather festive since the fair was held during the last weekend in November.

Step 1

I picked roast chicken out of the first day's list.

Step 2

This challenge was set by my little friend Sam Kerridge who became glued to the front of my stand and had to be tyre-levered away by his mum several hours later! Baby-sitting

other stallholder's children seems to have become one of my sidelines. I suppose I should consider it a complement that Sam became so familiar with my patter that he started repeating it for me. I could have left him in charge of the stand by the end of the day! Sam also helped me out by being my photographer, pressing the camera shutter for the oranges and cabbages pictures (shown below)

Step 3

Since the principles for making the Roast Chicken are already shown in my book Making Miniature Food I won't repeat them here. Just remember that a chicken is smaller and has a rather narrower breast than a turkey. Also the neck

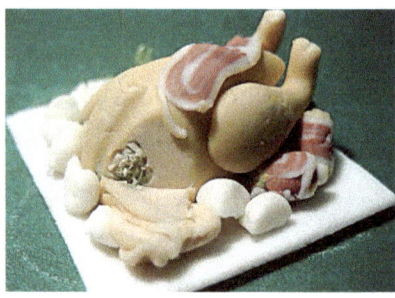

cavity is small so there isn't much room for stuffing. I added stuffing and bacon rolls just because I like them. The pictured chicken would need a coating of Humbrol Clear Colour to make it appear cooked like the turkey above. *[Humbrol Clear Colour may not be available now, so just use ochre and brown colour pastels or powder and varnish]*

Step 4

Mistletoe.

On the second day, at the last minute a very nice lady called Pam from Brightlingsea threw down this challenge which caught my imagination. I'm the sort of

person who buys a tool and then thinks what to do with it later. For instance the paint stirrers I bought from the Squires stall look like really good serving spoons at one end and oars at the other. Alternatively they will make really useful modelling tools.

Step 5

A few weeks earlier I'd tipped the contents of an icing nozzle set into my tool kit and I knew the very one that I was going to use for this project! I think it's for piping leaves or ribbons. It has an end which looks a little like a long, tiny teardrop. Just perfect for my Mistletoe leaves. I mixed the colour from leaf green and ochre.

Step 6

I extruded the stems using my clay gun.

Step 7

The berries are porcelain coloured Doll Fimo but you could use 75%

translucent to 25% white mix.

I cheated as much as I could and bought a strip of holly leaves from the Merry Gourmet Miniatures stand. The holly berries are seed beads on sale at the Tee Pee Crafts stand and the basket was one of C+D crafts'. I have to admit I couldn't mount this display on the day since the stems were so floppy, so I promised Pam I would send it on to her.

The oranges project is shown in full on my website angiescarr.co.uk and there are also links there to my YouTube videos of making oranges, bananas and cabbages.

Step 8

During the weekend my other demonstrations included oranges, cabbage canes (pictured) and bananas in both whole and the peeled variety.

Sandwich

Originally published in DHMS Magazine Issue 81 March 2001

Have We All Gone Mad!?

At Alexandra Palace fair last year My friend Gail (MGM) and I were musing on the sanity of ourselves as makers, and those of us who are collectors of all things tiny and outrageously detailed. If we're mad,

we decided, at least were the nicest kind of mad we know. And in fact we all seem to like each other. Something I regrettably can't say about the other mad world of musicians I occasionally inhabit. So, I was lying abed rather late last Saturday, trying to get started on yet another crazy project, While opening my letters I came across the following which tickled me so much I ended up almost in tears with my sheets scrunched up in my mouth. I just had to share it with you.

Gloria wrote:-

Dear Angie.
I have been given a doll's house kit and am turning it into a busy solicitors office. My Junior clerk is young Des Astor and he is well named [think about it!]. On his desk in amongst all the papers I would love to find a large succulent egg and bacon 'buttie', but I don't know how to go about it. (My waistline testifies to the amount of research I've done on the subject!)

I would like two thick slices of soft white bread with golden crusts, cut across the diagonal. One half is uneaten as yet, the dark crispy bacon slices are hanging out of each side and brown sauce is oozing from the cut edge in the middle. the other half is half eaten and egg yolk and brown sauce is dripping onto the greaseproof paper it was wrapped in - Excuse me, I will just pop into the kitchen and check my description is accurate........!

Can you help me please or do I need a doctor?

Yes Gloria (Good) you most probably do. Shall we get a joint appointment?

Step 1

I started by preparing a bread 'cane' for slicing. I used a mix of translucent and white Fimo (approximately 3 to 1) with a

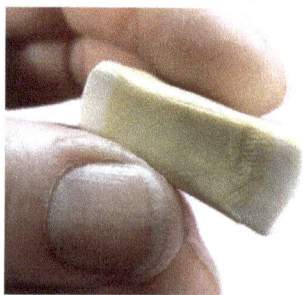

tiny piece of ochre just to take the sharpness off the white. This mix is formed into a box shape. Then wrapped with a slightly darker mix just by adding a really tiny piece of brown.

Step 2

This skin should be rolled and indeed pulled until it is as thin as possible.

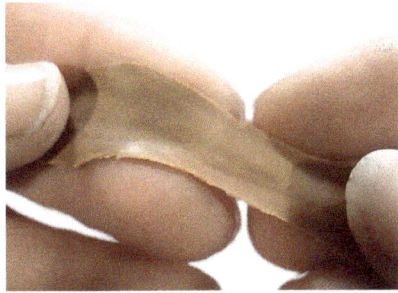

Step 3

The top is finished off with a really thin strip of a darker mix of ochre and brown with a little of the original mix. I left this cane to 'rest' and cool to make it easier to slice thinly without losing its shape.

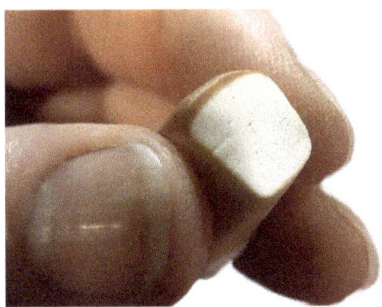

Step 4

The bacon is made using a stack of red meat coloured mix and ochre mixed with the translucent and white mix

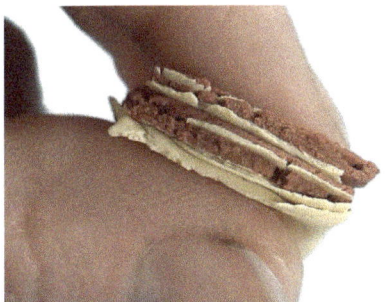

Step 5

this was lengthened and left to rest as well.

Step 6

Although the whole egg is not seen it doesn't hurt to make it up as a whole fried egg. That is with a thin base of white, the tiniest blob of golden yellow mixed with a little orange and a top of translucent.

Step 7

I then sliced the bread and the bacon and made my sandwich!

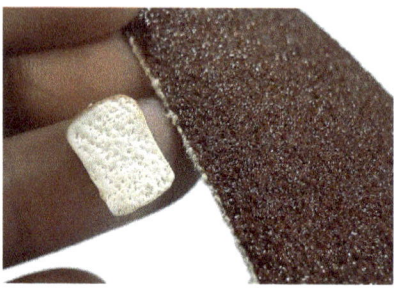

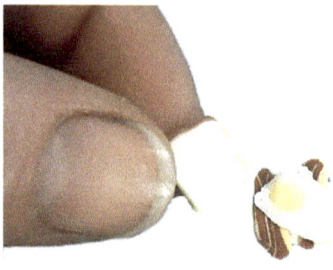

made using a smallish round ended cake icing nozzle.

Step 8

Remember to put a little of the yellow mix as well as a little brown paint or a sticky mix of brown Fimo (with Mix Quick) to finish the scene. *[Fimo Liquid has been invented since this challenge, so I would use this now, mixed with a little brown oil paint]*

Step 9

I then added the details only a really crazy (woman after my own heart) would think up. The diagonal cut, the couple of bites out of one side, The 'dribbly' bits of egg and brown sauce, and of course the couple of bites out of one half which I

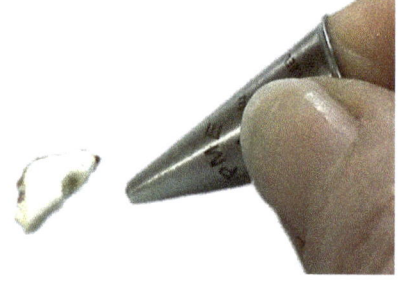

Step 10

Incidentally I opted for using tissue paper instead of a thin sheet of Fimo for the greaseproof paper. In this case as the level of detail in the sandwich is so great that the Fimo 'paper' would appear clumsy.

Red Cabbage

Originally published in DHMS Magazine Issue 82 April 2001

I may have been leading her astray!

A customer of mine rang me up recently wondering how she could make red cabbage. I wanted to sound clever I guess so I made the answer up on the spot. I was

a little worried when I came off the phone that I may have been leading her astray so I decided to make it this month's challenge.

When I saw him on T.V. recently, I was so impressed with the guy who carves miniatures in microscopic scales including a galleon in full sail on a match head, because his work makes mine look 'sane' and also because he speaks so articulately about his work. Apparently as he left the studio he whispered darkly to Richard Madeley 'You haven't seen the best of me yet'. Actually it probably wasn't darkly I just thought it sounded good.

One wonders what his next challenge might be. Maybe a dollshouse complete with tiny furniture on a pinhead? This type of miniaturisation is like climbing a mountain 'because it's there'. Although it is entirely possible to miniaturise items by caning methods down to minute scales, to achieve results you can actually see even in twelfth scale requires a compromise. This is partly because you can't physically make items like leaves thin enough for twelfth scale. And even if you could, you would be unable to see the result with the naked eye.

Also the size of the particles in your polymer clay then becomes an issue. The idea is to give the essence of the item you're making. It's like being a painter. You have to chose whether to be an impressionist, a super-realist, a surrealist or even a cartoonist (I think my crabs and lobsters are cartoon-like). When I make ordinary cabbages I make a cane with the veins of the leaves simply inserted into it in a lighter coloured clay which gives a sort of impressionistic effect. This is a compromise for visibility.

For these red cabbages I have used entirely different methods which give it a super-real look. I can get away with this because the contrast in red cabbage is so much greater than it is in green cabbages. In this project the colour becomes so thinned that particle size does begin to rear it's ugly head. In the Squid project in issue 76 the problem separation of clay particles was used to advantage to create a mottled surface colour. In this project this is something we want to avoid.

The one thing we just can't compromise on is colour mixing. It is absolutely essential to get a really strong purple colour for this project. I really do advise actually buying a red cabbage to take a really good look.

Step 1

Roll the purple out as thinly as you can. Add it to both sides of a thicker layer of translucent and white mix and roll again until you get really fine sheets. You will need two 'grades' one very fine. and one even finer!

A couple of tips for rolling really fine sheets is to use a straight sided glass bottle as a rolling pin, and a ceramic tile as a board to work on. Both your hands and the polymer clay need to be warm and scrupulously clean. However your tools need to be cool and absolutely dry.

If you roll only once in each direction and pick the material up and move it between each roll, just like pastry, you should avoid problems of the material sticking to the surface. Once it starts to stick it will continue to do so and you will have to clean everything and start again, so it is best avoided.

Of course the best, though rather expensive solution is to buy a Pasta maker for this type of work. Even so cleanliness is still the most important consideration since you are using two dramatically different colours. [This project was originally written when very few people used my methods for dolls house miniatures and so few would have a pasta machine or consider buying one. So I did not mention it. Obviously this is what I used to create these sheets]

Step 2

Make a tiny cone of the white colour.

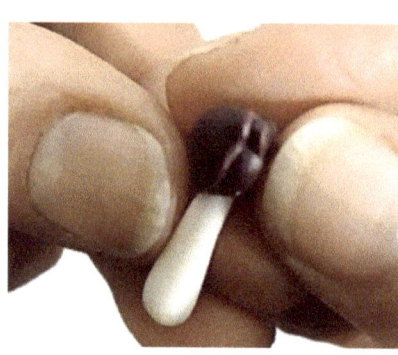

Step 3

Cut out a couple of circles from the thinnest clay. I've used an icing nozzle because it is a little blunt and has a tendency to 'seal' the two purple layers together as it cuts.

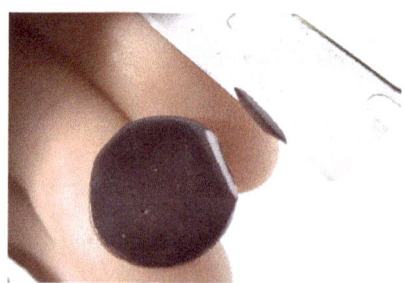

Step 4

You will need to further stretch these circles until they are as thin as you can possibly get them.

Step 5

You then add them to the end of the cone to form a sort of crumpled ball.

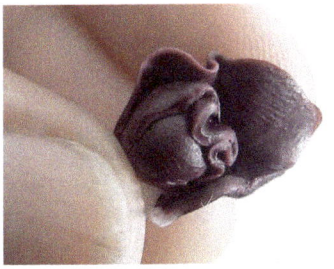

leaf veiner (there are several styles available on my website angiescarr.co.uk and some YouTube examples of using them too.).

Step 6

You then cut a couple of leaves from the slightly thicker sandwich. You need to cut the edge at an angle to expose some of the white and thin the leaf again but not near this white edge. The white bit should be added to the side of the cone as close to the top layer as possible, making sure the white of the leaf meets the white of the cone. Add another couple of leaves of the very fine and then start to build up outer leaves by using the thicker sheet and making several leaves which you press in a

Step 7

Oh, and in case you were wondering I checked the 'net' to make sure that red cabbages weren't an exotic brought in by some intrepid adventurer. I found if it had been brought to our shores it was more likely to be the Vikings. So, no worries about fitting in your dolls house no matter what era!

[I updated my methods subsequently to a caning method for multiple production. This project appears in my book Miniature Food Masterclass.]

Sweets

Originally published in DHMS Magazine Issue 83 May 2001

The Sweetest Things

Following Gloria's research for last month's challenge I thought I might do a little research myself for this month's challenge from Perry Lambert.

I've got a bit of a sweet tooth and I'm something of a chocoholic in fact, these

days, to quote my friend Dina, you could just about draw me just using circles! For those of you who share my passion for all things sweet and my concern for what it's doing to my waistline (not to mention my somewhat sedentary miniaturist's behind!) here is a challenge with very few calories and also surprisingly little frustration.

Ha except, that is, that my advice is usually to go out and buy the real thing so that you can work from life. Oh yes, my own little greed monster sent me off to the shops for the 'Allsorts' convincing myself that only by close inspection could I get those colours exactly right. It wasn't a long walk, certainly not long enough to burn off the 750 calories!

Have you noticed that the selection has changed over the years? I don't remember those little blobby jelly things coming in pink as well as in blue. The plain liquorice has changed to a flower shaped extrusion and there's a pink and liquorice battenberg type thing appeared recently. As well as good old Bertie Basset himself who has made an appearance in the form of a jelly baby in each pack. What is the world coming to?

You shouldn't make the mistake of putting Liquorice Allsorts(TM) into an early Victorian house or shop however, because a close inspection of the empty pack revealed that they weren't invented until 1899. So, probably best avoided in the pre-1900 house. And watch out for those changes if you're a purist. I couldn't find any miniature jars, although I know I've got some ... somewhere.

Step 1

I decided to make sweet bags. You could make these out of paper, but I

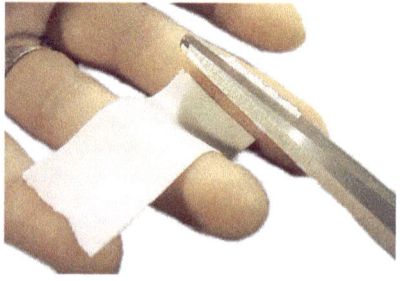

thought I'd have a go at polymer clay. My pasta maker rolls the thinnest of sheets but even I can stretch that even further. This does take practise, so expect a few torn sheets if you're a novice. To thin the clay out as far as it will go first roll it out as thinly as you can. Then smooth it lightly on both sides with your thumb on one side and forefingers on the other side of a fairly narrow sheet. This also gives the clay a nice sheen.

Step 2

As you can see from the illustrations I've used a little cling film wrapped around a pen to help me form the bag. The seam should be in the centre of the bag and not at the edges. I got it wrong at first attempt ... Yes, I usually do!

Step 3

The bottom is nipped together and the whole thing should be flattened gently on to the cooking surface.

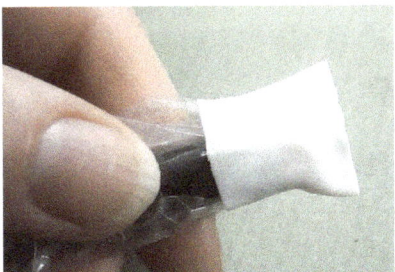

Step 4

The pen should then be removed followed, very gently, by the cling film. You can then arrange the top of your bag as if it is open, closed, falling over etc.

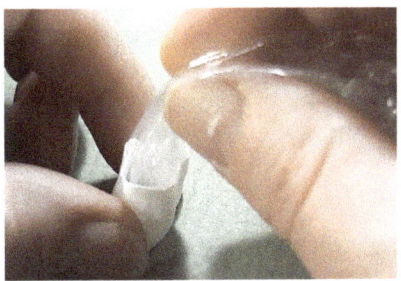

Step 5

The sweets are deceptively simple. The Humbugs, useful for earlier houses are just a small roll of white clay with even thinner strips of black stuck around the sides.

Step 6

The trick is to lengthen them a long way until the strip is really very thin indeed and then to cut the end off one way and

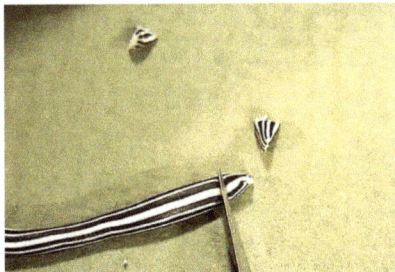

then turn the roll a quarter turn and cut the other way. This forms that 'tetra pack' sort of shape.

Step 7

There are three methods used for the allsorts. The coconut rounds in pink and yellow and the liquorice fondant cylinders are just simple canes where I wrapped one colour with another and lengthened them. Then cut into short lengths. The sandwiches were just that, a strip of black clay with two slightly thicker strips of the colour on the outside.

Step 8

You'll be surprised how thin you have to roll it for something like the correct scale. You may be able to see from the illustration with the coin that I have made these around 10th rather than 12th scale. The plain sandwiches were rolled on the thinnest setting on my pasta maker (which is very thin) and I rolled out the double decker ones by hand. They weren't quite the right thickness but the overall impression is good. You can cut the canes and then set the tiny sweets as you do with the humbugs, however I cut the sweets up while the clay is hot.

If you oven set your rolls and sheets and cut them while they are still hot from the oven take great care not to burn yourself. I use a flannel to hold the hot canes down with. Remember always to cut downwards and away from you. If the clay starts to cool and harden, stop cutting return them to the oven to re-heat. Cutting hard cold clay can be very dangerous. This is not something you should allow children to do.

Oh yes, nearly forgot the blue blobby things. They're just a tiny piece of blue clay, rolled on some very rough sandpaper and slightly flattened onto your baking surface.

Step 9

There are several tiny cutters available that you can use to make chocolates. I left these out of the project since I've misplaced my favourite tiny cutter which is a teardrop shape. My chocolate colour is a mixture of terracotta (now called chocolate) and green Fimo. *[A full colour mix table for various colours of chocolate in several brands of clay is available in my book Miniature Food Masterclass.]*

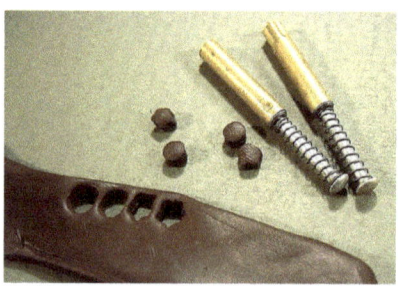

Tongue

Originally published in DHMS Magazine Issue 84 June 2001

N.B. This challenge has been slightly rewritten to make more sense in book format.

Here's a killer only for the really very patient!

Well, you did have it too easy last month didn't you? So here's a killer only for the really very patient! . This month my raw materials for investigation were a little hard to find. What with B.S.E. and Foot and Mouth etc., offal seems to have the awful smell of the things boiling for hour after hour. To be fair, I enjoyed the end result as much as anyone. Mind you he never could get me to try the 'babies nappies' (boiled tripe and onions).

Step 1

The Tongue is a rather complex cane. It is essentially made up of layers of slices from different stacks of colour. The colours you will need are:- translucent (for the Jelly), a basic meat mix made from terracotta (now called chocolate), red and

lost favour a little in the local butcher and supermarket. Even Sainsbury's seem to have ceased to stock ox tongue. Now I'm wondering whether it's on the 'prohibited' list. If so, all the more reason to commit it to memory in our doll's houses.

My dad (who was a gastronome of all things smelly and disgusting looking) pressed tongues at home. I well remember

translucent clay and translucent and white mixed with a very little of the meat colour just to take the brightness off the white.

Step 2

Think of each part of the whole as a separate element. A tongue has several areas of muscle and these appear as stripes of meat colour interspersed with a sort of creamy fatty substance (sounds awful doesn't it?) You have constantly to keep in mind the direction from which the finished cane will be seen. That is to say the 'grain', just like in wood, will look different when cut from different directions. If you want to see a line in the sliced end of a roll, you need to put it in as a strip. A short line would be a shorter strip. No, I'm just confusing you! You really do need to look at the real thing to make this for yourself.

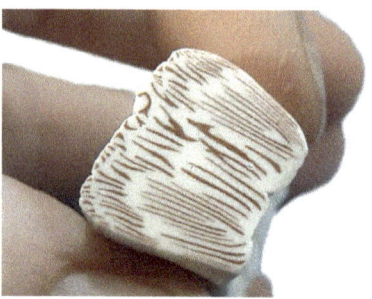

Step 3

Each section is made up of a stack or cane of it's own and these canes are layered (rather like the bacon project in my book Making Miniature Food and Market stalls)

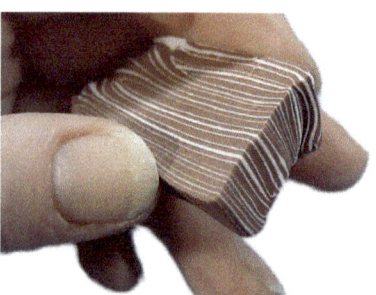

Step 4

The Jelly is laid down first

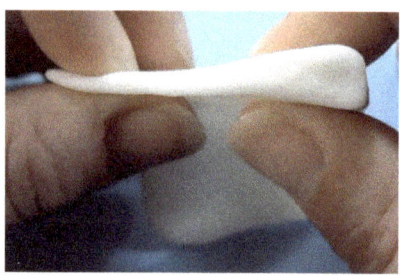

Step 5

and a thin strip of creamy colour (for the surface of the tongue)

Step 6

Slices from prepared canes are then built up.

Step 7

Finally the resultant stack is rolled and lengthened. This is very difficult and I certainly lose my way many times trying to remember which direction to lay stacks and canes in to get the right cross section.

Ah well, this series is, after all, called 'Challenge Angie' and not 'Ask Angie to make something really easy that she (and we) can knock off in ten minutes'. So, thank you for all your devilish challenges. *Please visit my website at angiescarr.co.uk for tips and updates.*

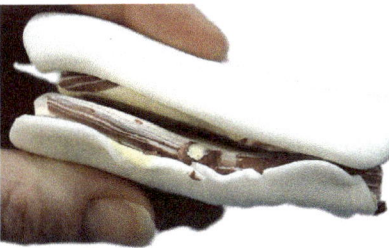

Step 8

I won't say I was perfectly happy with the result but the colours are about right. Next time I'll try harder!

Peppers And Pizzas

Originally published in DHMS Magazine Issue 86 August 2001

Where there's a will there's a way.

Here is a very interesting challenge from Bette Accola who regularly emails me from the United States. Bette says:-
'I love the ChallengeAngie articles you have in the Dolls House & Miniature Scene Magazine. I have a couple challenges for you, first how about a cuttable green pepper or green pepper cane to slice off pepper rings, second a cane of peach slices. I don't have a subscription yet, but I do order the magazines I want on on-line. Please help me if you can. I would love to have these slices to add to salads, etc.'

This is the kind of challenge that I really like. One which on the surface looks impossible. But, as they say, where there's a will there's a way. My first thought was to use a pair of cutters one slightly smaller than the other. I really couldn't find any that were entirely suitable. Mostly they are flower shaped and I needed something with less dramatic curves on the outside and extra 'flesh' on the inside preferably of a slightly different hue. The next idea was to make the peppers as a 'cane' but make the middle translucent. This wouldn't be very satisfactory because translucent clay is just that. Translucent, rather than transparent.

I finally hit upon the idea of using a central core which could be removed after cooking to form an entirely hollow cane. I tried several different ideas out including brass tubes and pre-made milliput formers. Everything stuck and nothing looked quite right.

(If you want to shortcut all this I sell pizza slices (and pepper canes too) on my website angiescarr.co.uk and there are also links there to YouTube videos of making pizza.)

Step 1

As usual I was pottering around the house doing something entirely inconsequential like building a back gate when the important breakthrough hit me. Knitting needles! It took me a few attempts using different sizes and numbers of needles and different thicknesses of material. Here is how to get the result which I think (so far) is most realistic.

Tightly tape together three or four metal (not plastic) knitting needles at the

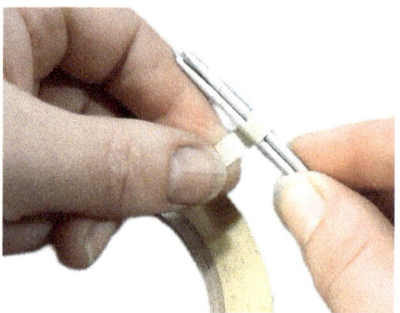

top and bottom using masking tape. Those without ends are best and they should preferably be 20cm needles or even smaller if you're using four. Ideally your needles will be fairly new and unscratched. You must use masking tape if you are to leave it on in the oven setting process. If you use another type of tape please remove it before you put your 'cane' in the oven.

Step 2

Make a mix of the colour you are using, in the example, I am using red for red peppers. You could have green, yellow or even orange peppers. Then divide this mixture in half. To one half add an equal amount fimo soft in the yellow translucent colour. or you could use a little yellow and a little translucent.

Smooth a little of this slightly lighter colour into the grooves between the needles. Pressing fairly firmly but without allowing the needles to part.

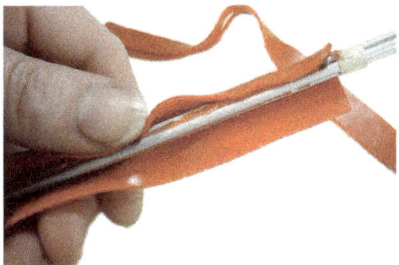

Step 4

Do the same with the other half leaving a slight gap in the middle. Experience has already taught me that if you make a single strip the whole length of the needles it is very difficult to remove later!

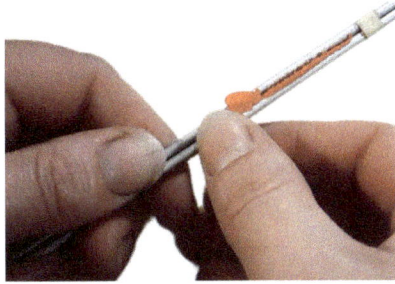

Step 3

Roll a very thin sheet of the darker colour and wrap this around one half of the needles, trimming off, and closing the edges together smoothing it gently to make the seam invisible and giving the whole thing a 'sheen'. *[I have updated this method and now put a layer of lighter colour on the main strip as well as between the needles.]*

Step 5

When the cane is cooked and cooled, pull the two halves apart with a firm even pull. The strip should come off slowly but reasonably easily. This is due to the coating on the needles.

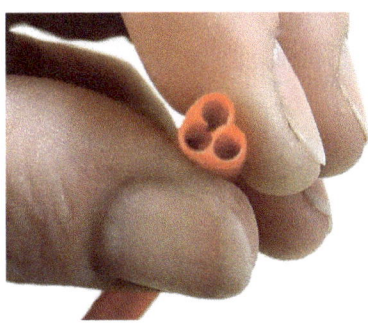

Step 6

Using a single sided blade or scalpel cut thin slices from this cane. Single sided blades can sometimes be bought from your chemist but let me know if you are having difficulty finding them as I have now found an alternative source of these elusive little beasties! If your cane crumbles easily return it to the oven and re-cook at a slightly higher temperature bearing in mind the safety instructions on the pack.

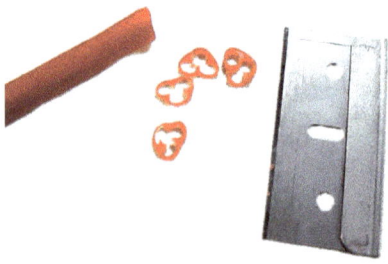

Step 7

To make the pizza you need to mix a cream mix which will do for both the base and the cheese. Try using half and half white and translucent with just a little ochre. The tomato mix is red and translucent yellow. *[This is another project where the invention of Liquid polymer clay makes an even more realistic effect for the toppings]*

Step 8

Alternative toppings for the pizza include pepperoni, onions, mushrooms and tomatoes all made by caning. and my cheat is olives, little black seed beads. Remember, for twelfth scale, a twelve inch pizza will be one inch in diameter. A family size just a little larger..... Yum!

Step 9

Incidentally the pizza cutter is simply a cocktail stick, split at one end with a small sequin inserted into it.

To make the peach slices Bette, I suggest you make a thicker peach coloured strip (remembering to mix in plenty of translucent) and wrap it around a single knitting needle. Score through the length of the the tube on both sides before oven setting. When you have pulled the cane off the needle warm the cane up again and gently separate the two halves. You should then be able to slice peach shaped slices off each half. To get the shape a little more realistic use a slightly diagonal cut and throw away every second piece.

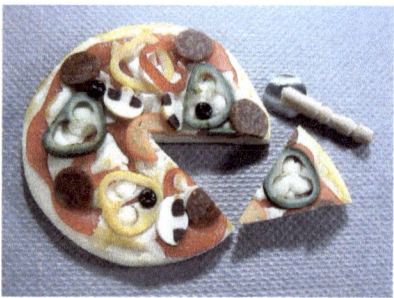

Tomatoes

Originally published in DHMS Magazine Issue 87 September 2001

Rather like seaside rock.

This challenge was set for me ages ago by Jean Brattan, a British 'ex pat', who, during the course of several emails it turned out came from my own home town of Hull. Not only that but she was brought up just a street away from my own. Later it transpired that her brother had lived two or three houses away from me and that I knew him! Doesn't this emphasise how small a world it is.

Anyway Jean, thanks for a challenge which clearly demonstrates how you can use caning to make incredibly realistic detail in an almost infinitely small scale. I often explain that these methods are rather like those a 'Seaside Rock' Maker might employ. This explanation left my class looking baffled recently. But then I was in Stockholm! It wasn't the language that was the problem. Most of them spoke 'better English' than a lot of Englishmen. It was just that they had never seen this rather British invention. And of course the word Millefiore means little to most people too. For those of you who are not familiar with my favourite method of working, the technique I employ for the tomatoes and a lot of my other work is now often called 'caning' by polymer clay enthusiasts, many of whom use it for jewellery making. Put very simply it is making a short fat cylinder from the colours and shapes you want to appear in the final cane, and then lengthening it to bring it down to a smaller scale. It means even people who's eyes are not as good as mine can be confident of good results even if they can't see them with their own naked eye.

When producing work which is going to be really tiny like this it is even more important to mix the colours exactly right. In these illustrations there are actually two versions of the same project in which the colours are slightly different. Whilst I'm very happy with the shape and definition of the second one, the colours look a little wrong. This is because I mixed some old clay in, and thought it would be more translucent than it was. The translucency is the most important aspect of this complex little cane. if you follow the ideas carefully and mix the colours from life you should get a pleasing result as long as you use plenty of translucent. It is worth remembering that the translucency is more obvious when the clay is cooked. Another important little tip is that you should make the seeds really obvious by slightly over-emphasising the colours. Subtlety won't work at this scale!

Step 1

the real ...

Step 2

and the cane. - For me the two are often approximately the same size before they are lengthened down to twelfth scale.

Step 3

I started by building up the seed area by making a teardrop shape of yellow with a little green round one edge.

Step 4

I then wrapped it with a very translucent wrapping with just a little tomato colour.

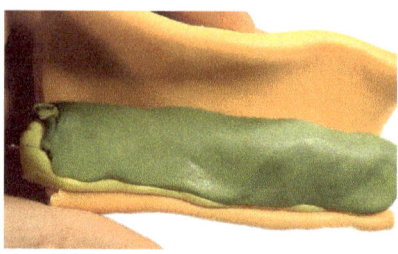

Step 5

I made up three sections like this one and separated them with a slightly more dense (and a little lighter) colour.

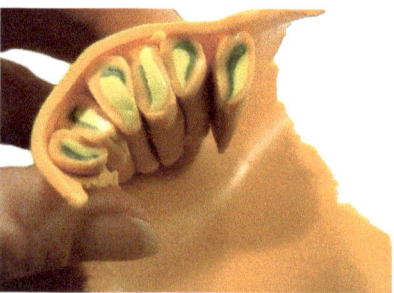

Step 6

Each section fitted together round a central core and was wrapped around with the second colour.

Step 7

The whole outside is wrapped with a dense tomato colour mix. By that I mean

There is more on caning tomatoes in my book Miniature Food Masterclass available from my website angiescarr.co.uk and there are also links there to YouTube videos on caning and enclosing canes to form whole, cut and peeled fruits.

there is no translucent added to this outside skin, but it is very thin.

Step 8

It really is important that you mimic nature as closely as you can so that when you reduce the cane down to its final scale it is as naturalistic as possible.

Moulded Fish

Originally published in DHMS Magazine Issue 88 October 2001

Sardines in crates quick sharp.

This Challenge was set for me by Sheila Rochambeau who, from what I can understand makes weird and wonderful Backgammon sets using miniatures as playing pieces. Sheila is mourning the loss of The Singing Tree (as are many of us) and needed some sardines in crates quick sharp. I told her this would be a challenge, given my shortage of time...And so it is!

Things have gone a bit 'mouldy' this month. Since my crazy attempt to cover the entire surface of the planet with miniature lemon slices, starting with my living room floor and continuing through my bedroom (including in my bed for Pete's sake) and out of the door into the street, well I've rather gone off 'caning'. For those of you new to this column 'caning for miniaturists' isn't some form of small scale perversion as suggested by one of my cheekier customers, but a process by which you make big patterns ... into little ones, rather like in seaside rock. Ah well, If you want to know more about that you'll have to wait 'till next month because I've got right into Moulds.

I also discovered this stuff a few months ago during the jelly project. The two part silicone moulding paste can be bought from several sources. My first one was the Gedeo brand which I originally bought in the craft section of my local DIY Superstore. Since I bought it when the store was closing down I couldn't find it again in Hull. Now I find this stuff called Silicone Plastique thanks to a kind lady called Susie from QH designs (a cake craft supplier). I've been fiddling around with it to find out what other uses I could put it to.

[I now use Minitmold, another silicon paste, available from my website angiescarr.co.uk for most of my moulding, as it sets in about 10 minutes and doesn't need a release agent, other than a little talcum powder to make the second part of a mould.]

Silicone Moulding paste is a similar material to that used by dentists to take an impression of your teeth. It follows that this stuff takes up the finest detail and the moulds you make remain flexible so that you can even have slight 'undercuts' (I'm not sure if that's the right word). The other benefit of making moulds is you can make impressions of your best work and repeat them over and over again. The material comes in two parts and you simply mix them together in equal quantities and press the mix over your 'master' and allow it to set!

Step 1

For Sheila's sardine crates I made just one fish and created a mould from it. The original fish is made using a combination of simple geometric shapes. Although you don't have to make the head from a separate diamond shape I find it does help to get the shape right. I made this one in red with the extra parts in black just so you could see how I put it together. Incidentally the texture was an impression from one of my tool handles

Step 2

I then made lots of little fishies from the first mould and piled them up on top of each other. To shortcut the process even further I then made another mould from the resultant pile.

Step 3

I had sixteen boxes to make, plus a few more for my web customers so the next process took some time. A soft mix of dark coloured polymer clay works best, pressed firmly into the mould. I used one shade of metallic powder as a release agent, brushed into the mould. The other shades were brushed on to the moulded but uncooked fish to make them look more three dimensional and iridescent. I found the Holly Products pearl powder particularly suitable for this. The fish piles can now be cooked. *[since writing this article I've found using a lighter colour material for the fish actually gives a better result. But the best result of all comes from using a shaded cane ... see my book* Making Mniature Food *or my Youtube fish project, links on my website]*

The boxes were made by a neighbour of mine to my specifications. He started dying them with a mahogany wood stain but we were happier with a mid oak stain in the end. This was to give the impression that the boxes had seen some use.

I threaded some dirty brown coloured button thread through drill holes in the ends of the box from the inside, tying the ends together inside the box and leaving just enough slack to form handles after the 'ice' was placed in the bottom.

Step 4

I did try the toughened safety glass approach, that is to say using broken windscreen glass. I'm assured that this works but please don't make the mistake that I did of trying to break down larger pieces (mine was from a vandalised bus shelter) I found to my cost that this stuff can still cut! I decided to make a mould for this process as well. To make a 'master' for the ice I cooked a little Fimo pressed inside the box. I then removed this section from the box and glued on some more Fimo which I'd oven set *on the crumbly side* and chopped into fine chunks. (* cook at a lower temperature and only for a short time*)

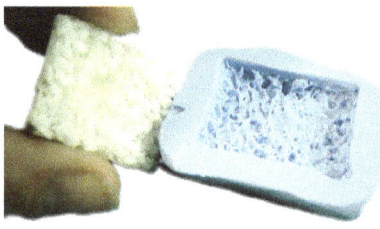

Step 5

When the glue was dry I made an impression with the moulding material squashed straight down on to it. I have glass surfaces in my workshop which make this easy but you can use a plate or ceramic tile. Realistic ice was made by pouring clear casting resin into the resultant mould. I did find the resin took a little longer to cure than I had expected so when I damaged one in the attempt to remove it from it's mould I chopped the soft resin up and stuck some on top of the fish.

Step 6

Actually you can't see the ice underneath at all but you would see anything that didn't look right, that's Murphy's law and my abiding principle! You could also use this idea for producing crushed ice surfaces for fish shops etc.

Strawberries

Originally published in DHMS Magazine Issue 89 November 2001

... or Jordgubbe

I knew it wasn't going to last long, this avoidance of 'caning' for miniaturisation. You see, amazing natural phenomena like the strawberry just get the creative juices going!

hosts took me for a meal on one of the beautiful little islands which make up the city of Stockholm. The meal was fantastic, the company warm and welcoming and the chatter very amusing. At the end of the meal we all opted for the strawberries which, I have to admit weren't Swedish.

I don't remember having more than one glass of wine, (though I did forget the warnings about the price of drinks in Sweden and also had a cocktail.) Maybe it was this which loosened my tongue. When I commented how delicious the strawberries were one of our company threw down the challenge of making a cut strawberry. I should have smiled sweetly and slapped down my natural urge to please (or was it arrogance) but oh no, I said 'I can do that! I wasn't quite sure how and I started waffling on about planes and dimensions. Well that was it. Too late!

On my website angiescarr.co.uk there are also links to YouTube videos of making strawberries.

Step 1

My new friend Ma Lou had heard me and arrived at the workshop the next day with a punnet of beautiful large strawberries. Large ... but not large enough. The problem is that you can miniaturise just about any pattern using 'canes' but there comes a scale beyond which you can't actually see the detail with the naked eye. And so it is with true twelfth scale, cut

This group of miniaturists could be any nationality. But you can tell we're in Sweden. How?

A few months ago I spent a few days in the beautiful city of Stockholm in Sweden. I was there to do some workshops but I must admit that my memories of the trip are more those you would expect to bring back from a holiday. While I was there my

strawberries. So I guess I wriggle out of this one by suggesting that 'twelfth is not the only scale' and hope you enjoy the process. If you're a hardened twelfth scaler you could apply it to something larger than this tiny fruit.

Step 2

Sue Heaser taught me the 'Skinner shade' technique which is so called because it was 'invented' by Judith Skinner. By using this method you can achieve gradient colours and in combination with other

caning techniques you can come up with stunning results. The idea is a simple mathematical one but don't worry if you don't understand maths! Basically if you put two triangles of different colour together …

Step 3

and keep folding and rolling in the same direction …

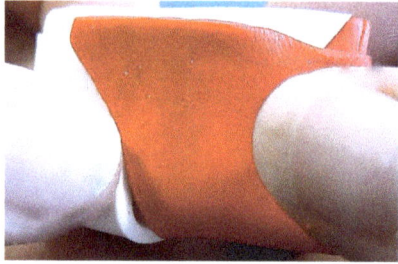

Step 4

you can achieve a perfect blend of colour through from one to the other. In my strawberry cane I used red through to a white and translucent mix.

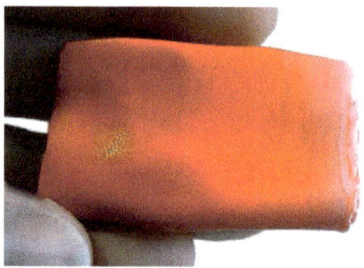

Step 5

I folded the resulting shaded sheet up and then squashed it back in the other direction

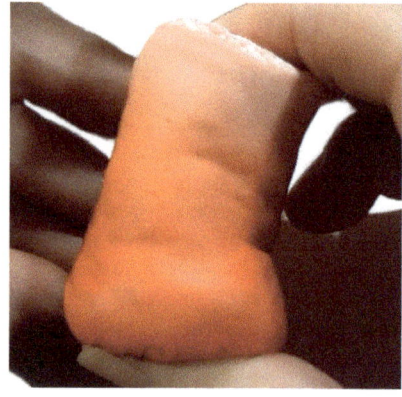

Step 6

and lengthened it producing one side (without the centre) of the strawberry.

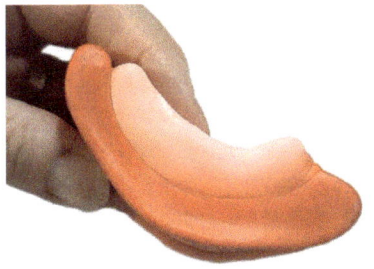

Step 7

The blade I used to cut into the side section is a tissue blade which you can get from the polymer clay pit. I used this blade, rather than my usual single sided blade, because I wanted a slight curve in my cut.

Step 8

I then added white strips into the sections and closed it all back up again.

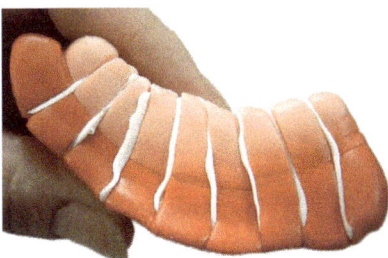

Step 9

I only made one half and lengthened that until it was long enough to cut into two as I wanted an exact mirror image. The colour in the very centre is Fimo soft translucent red.

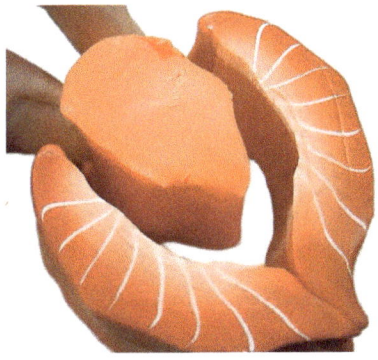

Step 10

The resultant large cane is then 'stretched' down to as small as you can get away with and still see the detail. You can get down to twelfth scale but you'll need a magnifying glass to see the results. I did explain to my Swedish hosts that making canes is rather like making seaside rock, but they just stared at me blankly.

Anyway Ma Lou, I'm sending you your miniature strawberries and also some Bridlington rock and some seaside rock with a strawberry design running through it. Is seaside rock just a British tradition? Let us know. And while you're at it, why not try making miniature seaside rock? I'll "pass" on Bridlington, but you could try Rhyll!

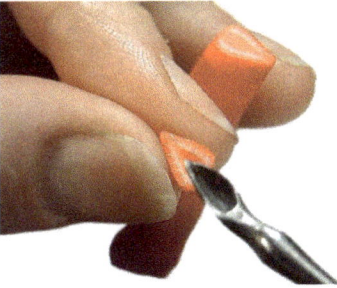

Acknowledgements

Among many others:-

Gail and Aileen Tucker

Birdy Heywood

Alex Curtis (now Blythe)

Sue Heaser

Sam Kerridge (photographs of orange and cabbage canes on 'Live at Ally Pally')

and for constant support over the years:-

Margaret Curtis

Nicola Croad

Cilla Halbert and Pär

And my lovely and supportive husband, (boss … and slave) Frank Fisher who edits all my pictures and text, and is the protagonist behind all my published work including this collection.

Apologies to the hundreds of friends and customers who's names I couldn't fit here but who's support is consistent and always very much appreciated.

Contact details for magazines featured

Dolls House and Miniature Scene Magazine
www.dollshousemag.co.uk

Dolls House Projects
www.dollshouseprojects.co.uk

Dollhouse Miniatures Magazine (USA)
www.dhminiatures.com/

The Dolls House Magazine
www.thegmcgroup.com/

Index

Alexandra Palace	35		Milliput	18,22
Allsorts	44		Minitmold	18,22,56
Anglo Saxon	11		mistletoe	36
artichokes	28		Mix Quick	12,18,24,33,40
bacon	39		mould	18,22,56
bags	44		mushy peas	26
berry	36		mussels	33
boar	8		net	13
bread	38		olive	31
butter	26		paella	31
cabbage, red	41		pasta machine	42
caning	14,19,47,54,60		peach	52
cheese	52		peppers	50
chicken	35		pheasant	14
chips	26		pine cone	30
chocolate	46		pineapple	17,29
claygun	36		pizza	50
coleslaw	25		potato	25
cutter	10,36,42,46		powder	57
eggs	22		resin	58
extrude	36		rice	33
eye	14		sandwich	38
feather	15		sardines	56
Fimo Liquid	24,40		Scenic Water	24
fish	56		seed	54
fries	26		sieve	28
glass	58		Skinner shade	60
glaze	10		squid	20
Humbrol	10,18,36		strawberry	59
humbugs	45		sweets	44
ice	58		tapas	31
knitting needle	50		tissue blade	61
leaf	10,36,43		tomato	53
Liquid Fimo	24,40		tongue	47
liquorice	44		Tudor	8
lobster	11		varnish	21
marble	21		Victorian	44
mash	26		Viking	43
medieval	8		wicker	8
mesh	28			

www.ingramcontent.com/pod-product-compliance
Ingram Content Group UK Ltd.
Pitfield, Milton Keynes, MK11 3LW, UK
UKHW020244240426
12048UKWH00026B/1591